MADE IN CAPTIVITY

For Chiara,

Best wishes,

Nick Pearson

MADED IN CAPTIVITY

✦

Nick Pearson

10/8/11

OFFA'S PRESS
2011

First published 2011 by Offa's Press
Ferndale, Pant, Oswestry, Shropshire, SY10 9QD

ISBN: 978-0-9565518-2-5

Copyright © Nick Pearson

The right of Nick Pearson to be identified as the author of this work has been asserted by him in accordance with the Copyright, Designs and Patents Act 1988.

Typeset in Baskerville Old Face

Designed by Début, Wolverhampton

Printed and bound by Steatham Colour Printers, Wombourne, Staffordshire

This book is sold subject to the condition that it shall not, by way of trade or otherwise, be lent, re-sold, hired out, or otherwise circulated without the publisher's prior consent in any form of binding or cover other than that in which it is published and without a similar condition including this condition being imposed on the subsequent purchaser.

Acknowledgements

Acknowledgements are due to the editors of the following publications in which versions of many of these poems first appeared: *The Affectionate Punch, Assent, Avocado, Breakfast All Day, Brittle Star, Envoi, Haiku Quarterly, The Interpreter's House, Manifold, The North, Poetry & Audience, Poetry Nottingham, Pitch, Prop, Raw Edge, The Rialto, Smiths Knoll* and *Staple*.

A number of these poems were also published in the following anthologies: *Buzz* (Templar Poetry, 2009), *Haiku for Lovers* (MQ Publications, 2003), *Wolverhampton Write Now* (Wolverhampton Libraries, 2003), *New Writings from Wolverhampton* (Wolverhampton Libraries, 2010) and *Wenlock Poetry Festival Anthology* (Ellingham Press, 2011).

'Cavern of Cloth' was awarded a prize in the Yorkshire Open Poetry Competition, 2009.

'Receivership' was nominated for the Forward Prize in 2010 (Best Single Poem category).

Contents

Clothing Item	9
The Arrival	10
Receivership	11
Early June Sun	12
A Clean Well Lit Place	13
News	14
Made in Captivity	15
Referential Upbringing	16
Office Women on Wet Days	17
Coming Clean	18
Headhunted	19
Short Shrift	20
Silent Apple	21
Lapworth Museum Stillborn	22
La La La	23
In Praise of Brindley Place	24
Historic Market Town	25
A Lidl E Berlin	26
Industrial Hill Towns	27
Heritage Town	28
Shorts	30
Do the Right Thing	31
Holiday to Remember	32
Film Noir Night Class	33
Cavern of Cloth	34
Nobody Dies	36
Shallow Grave	38
Babbage Hardcore	39
Who Do You Think You Are?	40
A Father's Trousers	41
Driving Back Home I Remember Wicklow	42
Dirty Car	43
Distance Learning	44
Blessed	45

Before & After	46
Somewhere South	47
Entitlement	48
Escalator	49
Gap	50
On Harrison & Dearborn	51
Change	52
Young Girl Alone	53
Tell It How It Is	54
Six Notes	55
Dwellings	56
Outings	57
Personal Stuff	59
Day Trip	60
Audit Team	61
Final Frame	62

Clothing Item

Just when he thinks it's gone
the obsession is back,
grips him at lunch time,
like it always does,
on the way to M&S
for a calorie counted
Mex Tex tortilla wrap:

single pleated
one hundred percent cotton
classic cut
chinos,
beige,
thirty-four,
long:

their mercerised folds draw him
through the shop's aperture,
he buries his nose
in the fresh-stock lustre
of their weave.

Nemesis: another pair.

At home they hang heavy over shoes,
the pockets have no depth.
In *Cut and Trust* the machinist
says to leave well alone,
but he insists an inch here,
an inch there,
tells her "just do it."

Ruined,
he wears them for a week in private
like a fool.

The Arrival

The arrival of the jacket
was a little flash in time.
It was the armour I awoke
in the night thinking of.
I thought it good enough
to be my natural shroud.

I dreamt I wore my jacket
with the cellophane on,
in the same manner,
and for the same purpose,
as three piece suites
are left covered in a lounge.

Each night it hung wrapped
on the wardrobe door,
cool fibres stretching downwards,
drape revitalising for another day.
And on those bright days
I marvelled again.

Receivership

I had a face-off once about a take-away coffee
with that dark haired woman. I asked for hot milk
in an Americano and she said I wanted a Cappuccino,
which I didn't, I wanted a white Americano, and she said
that one always came black and she knew all about coffees,
was I accusing her of not knowing all about coffees?
Of course, she had her audience: that soft-faced supervisor
and tin badge-breasted young Natalie, hard as they come
with her made up stare slashing up the precinct traffic.
Watching her serve while waiting to be served
I used to wonder whether it was the job or the people or both
that fixed everything in that face glaze of middle distance,
the one that said there never had been, and never would be,
any new wave customer care flies on her (forget that crap).
Was retail a choice she'd made at sixteen or seventeen or a vocation
for which she'd stood in a queue of dead women's shoes
until she was called to the counter of the Six Buns Bakery,
the queue the learning, the shoes the skills, the counter the therapy
for a life I can only stereotype in this cap-brute, cake hungry town?
It doesn't matter now anyway, that question, because it's all gone
as I come to push the glass door for the free cup on my loyalty card
and find the door doesn't push and a sign on the glass saying
In Administration. There are letters skimmed across the mat,
cloths, rubber gloves, polystyrene cups and their lids, stock books,
slices of cheese sweating through their wrappers, a stainless steel ladle
all randomly fallen to places as if after some zero gravity experiment.
A huge bright poster of a potato stuffed with baked beans and butter
shields some of this floor show played out behind walls of glass,
and a small felt-tipped card announces that the cake of the week
is once again the Viennese biscuit with fake cream filling, and jam.

Early June Sun

You can fit about six buggies
and half a dozen teenage mums
in the tattooist's over the road.

All day there was a steady flow
from the new tree and bench
just outside this window.
First they would clump
in threes or fours or fives,
shouting each other's names,
sharing trays of orange chips.
Then they would be drawn over,
in a traffic defying charge
push across the fried egg island
to the den of ink and flesh.

Once inside I could see them
crowding up against a wall
covered in black patterns.
Some would come out again
to smoke on the pavement
and mouth back through the glass.

All day there was a smell
of ground opened beneath tarmac,
the sort that comes in summer
just as it begins to rain.

A Clean, Well Lit Place

In the High Street Grill
the daughter takes my order
and her father prepares the fish.
"A beautiful piece," he says, "no bones."

restaurant spelt backwards
in joined up red neon
hangs against the window,
hot amber compartments
glow with battered bits.
Outside, January gives nothing.

People come and wait and go,
a few sit at tables and order.
"Yours will be a few more minutes," she says.
I have to fancy chips:
I fancy her, too.

In the car
vinegar and salt brand my tongue,
a haddock falls open in my lap.

News

Mauled and manhandled over the miles,
creases fragile and seams unseaming,
it rested against my door's frosted glass,
your US Mail Global Priority parcel.
The printed customs label declared it
a *pre-worn pale green evening dress*,
so open, precise and clear a thing
as it shot the slow, wide arc of Earth.

Postmarked Oakland
two days after you'd moved on
I thought how you'd never owned a dress before,
that this now was the first one,
and how inside its envelope it was like a pillow,
soft, something to rest a head against.

Made in Captivity

Dolphins are the only animals
that really look like themselves
as souvenir models on a shelf:

slicked, plastic,
a neck-head umbilical plughole
where they were snatched wet
from some manufacturing process.

In the zoo shop
they densely fill three baskets -
baby, medium and large.
My hand churns their satisfying bulk.
Breed, breed, it says. Collect, collect.

Referential Upbringing

I was confused by words
as a child
living literally
as I did
in a literate family.
First there were the Janes,
Eyre and Austen,
not so plainly
fact or fiction.

Then came Emily,
Charlotte,
the whole Bronte family.
They lived in Bronte Country,
home of the Brontosaurus,
where fossils were found
on heaths, in cliffs.

One summer
we visited Yorkshire
in the Austin A40.
Tony Christie,
his hair like a pad of Brillo,
was singing in the charts
about going to Amarillo.
Which is in Texas,
like Austin.

Office Women On Wet Days

probably think they look a mess
when they come back from lunch,
hair challenged by invading winds,
dented, spoke-buckled umbrellas
in their damp, efficient mitts.

They slip breathlessly backwards
after blood-racing dash
into warm, embracing rooms:
moisture spotting make-up,
clothes shot with freshness,
complexions close and clear,
surprise rescinding years

caught off guard, unprepared.

Coming Clean

At my annual development review
I observe my boss has a new notebook:
bright cover, spiral bound,
sections for each responsibility.
He explains that he bought it himself,
with his own wages,
but that wouldn't suit me.

I tell him I like to take stuff
from the stationery cupboard
and throw it from my moving car
into the countryside at night.
Take, drive, throw: I have to do it.
The mixing of fresh air and speed,
stolen office supplies and fields
meets a need that's hard to explain.

He doesn't believe me.
I tell him I'll take him one night
to where a Pritstick fell.

Headhunted

Recruited externally to a new post,
Goldenboy arrived sporting the shiny
fibre mix of his own reputation.
Eyes perceptibly sunken by things he'd seen,
a kiss of gel along thirtysomething hair,
he held councillors in the palm of his hand,
proved himself shit hot with the new IT.

Proactive was the work style then,
running the distance, getting things done.
A breed apart in local government
he stalked the backroom stillness,
a smouldering touch torching dead wood,
New Order blazing the civic skyline.

A helluva-nice-guy, too, by all accounts:
ran a local blues club, organised family
fun nights, had an awesome office wit.
Always read what he called the *Grauniad*,
passing on a world's clever highlights
to wide-eyed, coffee-bright clerks.

But in the end some things never change,
someone always takes the rap for overspend.
And the scenario is tried and trusted:
redeployment to the margins of a structure,
union consultation on right of appeal;
that unexplained long-term sick leave,
a spectacular early pension deal.

Short Shrift

Our boss knows what goes on,
that we get in for nine,
rather than open at nine,
that we knock off again at eleven
to fetch toasties and cobs.
She's caught us answering calls
in an internal voice
without the McJob customer spiel,
and she's clocked all our unread e-mails
with her super-snooper know-how.
Married to the job,
company through and through,
the mission statement's her favourite meal.
In prissy head girl heaven
she'll take an apple for the preacher.

Nobody, and I mean nobody,
should have to put up with how she speaks to them,
like something from the heel of her shoe.
She thinks there's going to be changes,
that we're going to *share* our ideas with her,
move things along together.
Now please tell me if I'm wrong,
but what I want to know is this:
since when was I paid to think for managers?
In the other branches she's altered duties,
introduced flexible breaks,
installed a chilled water machine.
But it won't work down here:
when she comes to us with her plans
we'll be ready,
we'll have her.

Silent Apple

The crispness and noise of office lunchtimes
with their snap of Tupperware salad,
rustle of rice cakes and rasp of pots,
causes me to notice even more
the solitary reader with his silent apple:
a Cox or James Grieve, maybe,
aged a lifetime by its existential thump,
those days on shadow-grass,
nights of animal voices, the wheel of stars.

Lapworth Museum Stillborn

You contradict your own being,
erase a shining path
the living would have you swim.

Had you left Ichthyosaur mom
to thrash for just a second
in that Jurassic broth

you may have proved some point,
if only that paddles of flesh
could let you be fast master

of underwater roll and pitch.
But you are un-sprung,
snapped within the fossil map,

your platter-set softening snout
and huge, spoon-cold eye
already extinct.

They can see these things,
palaeontologists,
the deadest amongst the dead,

but in this Edwardian cabinet ship
of creaking ancestral certainties
we are twice cheated,

twice preserved from each other:
you in your unlived sea-stone self,
both beyond this plate of glass.

La La La

I want my poems to be like Kylie,
perfect parcels of song and sensuality
legging it down the page
with kick and push
of a band on cue,
an audience thumped up on love.

I want my poems to be like Kylie,
metaphor cute and image pert,
a dress change in every verse.
I want the years of soaped-up similes
to strut their time-served breeding,
cavort conceits like burdens of love.

I want them to swoon their words,
give just enough without letting go.
Put up and put down,
made up and made over,
with clever teeth and eyes that love,
I want my poems to be like Kylie.

In Praise of Brindley Place

Everyone loves a fountain,
a feature of wetness
to make them squeal or laugh.

It shoots out of steps here
like Roman water candles,
bubbling stalagmites

that grow a million years
every two minutes
then collapse back to stone.

Born to be Bored it says
on a young teenager's top,
but just for a moment she isn't

as her mother stops to snap
her beaming picture
against spray-burst and blue.

Between the heavy water hall
of the Sea Life Centre
and the canal's slow-cut flood

alongside eateries and bars
there is this small leak to freedom:
an agile, luculent garden

of withering, growing shoots
sprung beneath a city's glass,
its reach of towering sky.

Historic Market Town

In warm weather
young men walked the town
wearing thick old shirts,
their ties tight to the neck,
sweat bristling beneath jacket's wool.
If you looked at them
they would meet your eyes.

In the pubs, and there were many,
five hundred year old ghosts
elbowed a nicotine light of afternoons
playing maliciously
with the reception of free view channels.

Young women, perfect in their paleness,
spent the days parading
flagged streets and squares
with a curve of motherhood,
their infants fretting buggy straps,
babbling a memory
of outlawed hill-speak.
Each day after school
in the backs of shops and kitchens
children sliced local meat
with sharpened power tools.

Fires burnt along the sides
of disused quarry roads.
The sons of fathers raced their cars
around old craters,
abandoning them to algae's slow fingers
in angular pools of bitter,
un-blown water.

When rain fell
it turned the town's stone black,
washed through its intaglio
like etcher's acid.

A Lidl E Berlin

In a crammed corner of the store
you search for water without fizz,
inspecting tiny coloured print
on bottles torn from multi-packs.

I can't forget that we are lost,
overheat from lack of language.

A cashier scans your bubbles
and when we are outside again
the street is still an unknown street,
but one we have lived in just a little.

Industrial Hill Towns

Some of us feared such places
growing up in the Seventies,
their brutish, bronchial smog
swirling with muscled arms
out to break your back
for a face that looked like school.
Long red buses
bearing their names
passed along our high street
like black ships to hell,
went the other way
to where we'd set our sights.

Driving through one now
with a wide April sky
my car pin-balls around
bollarded brick streets
in search of the free car park.
The door steps of the houses
are as huge as vans,
scrubbed up like teeth
long out-grown their mouths.
There's not much to see:
shuttered precinct shops,
cap-and-brand teenage boys
cursing each other with spit;
in the toddlers' play park
some girls texting on swings.

All those years this place,
the slummed-in narrowness
of everything that was set
to skim its hump of earth,
and me not knowing.
Time has perked it from history,
and the buses, smaller, yellow
still come sometimes.

Heritage Town

Here is a grime-eaten, rain-fouled place,
the product of an industry's drab art,
etched along workshop and worker lines,
then pigeon-pecked by economic cycle
to some socially engineered mistake
of charity shops, sex shops and fish and chips.

Progress is a road that still harshly chips
at a people's parochial sense of place,
at their true right or their truest mistake.
Moving with the times is not an easy art,
even as cars replace the pavement bicycle
and electric trams run along re-laid lines.

The rooting instinct and old mating lines,
with palliatives of cake and fish and chips,
have locked them to a profitless cycle.
That here's better than any other place
is a history built from craftsmen's art,
the enamelled lure of a great mistake.

Two decades ago another great mistake
signed their sorry names to dotted giro lines,
forged an underclass from economics' art.
This town's heart and soul truly had its chips
when imports from every cheap foreign place
stalled the factory shift and furnace cycle.

Boys and girls feel the pull of a dull cycle
years after planners ploughed the mistake,
planted burgers and retail in its place.
A work ethic along hard and macho lines
is now a shared bench with bags of chips,
perspectives of steel-sculpted high street art.

Those without cash, influence or an art
embrace the horizons of a vicious cycle.
What's known and what isn't condemn chips
off the old block to live block's mistake,
to park their lives on bright double yellow lines
and look in, not out, from this greasy place.

Here is where they recycle the used mistake,
a place where grim extrusions become art,
where old chips on the shoulder are lifelines.

Shorts

Bright star –
pillow's
earring

The stiffness
in a parting
hug

Next day
your car parked
on a higher level

Rooms
keep the truth
of absence

This night
your answering machine
unplugged

Never untidy
all the cards from him
in date order

Autumn dusk –
a bridge's
fragile arc

Do the Right Thing

It's my fault,
I encouraged the interest,
which is why I find myself again
dodging a neighbour's security sensors
in the sub zero back garden
for a telescope session with my daughter.

Real science isn't all that big,
in fact Saturn is just a shaking blob
and the Crab Nebula empty black sky,
not an exploding fireball or crustacean.
Constellation mythology holds
interest for a while until Gemini,
with its twin stars Castor and Pollux,
suddenly gives her the hump.
Eleven years earlier she was herself
the victim of a multiple birth.

Humming into her fleece
on the edges of the dark lawn
she broods on what it means
to do the right thing:
how it doesn't have to be this hard,
her sister inside on the Gameboy.

Holiday To Remember

His daughter suffers womanhood,
hides first new aches,
her small pads pushed to the bottom
of a Nike shoulder bag.

Up early each day
fresh from the shower
she hates him with hurtful words,
pushes wide the gap
well laid plans of love and openness
sought to seal.

She'll never tell him why
the world has to change -
although, of course, he knows.
Fingers in her ears
mouthing *lah de dah de dah*
this summer will last forever.

Film Noir Night Class

It came in a big brown cardboard box,
they put it on the table in front of me,
my own personal file, on the first day.

Heavy as the largest large print bible,
the covers sealed in white laminate,
I carried its weight against my chest.

During weekly workshops it lay open,
chapters slopping against one another,
each falling page a bright, leftover meal.

Then through my letterbox came papers,
missing parts to give the whole a sense.
The steel lever creaked and snapped.

There is something for me to write now
and I reach into a box become lead.
The file burns hot, wants to destroy me.

I am the stone-blonde in that old classic,
I lift the lid of the great *wotsit*,
sear the universe with a vast whisper.

Beyond me on the night's surf-edge
Mike Hammer spools his stupid, ugly life;
at his back a beach house guts with light.

Cavern of Cloth

You have to go into Barnes Brothers
at ground level, grope a garment,
and then you're on their radar,
then you've entered the banter game.
"I've just put the shirts in order,"
the one with the wide grin
and monkey teeth confides,
"small, medium, large and fat bastard."
The items I hold for dry cleaning
bring the lad with glasses from suits
to escort me to a leather topped desk
in the department for larger men.
He shakes out my trousers,
checks the pockets, attaches a slip,
tells me they'll be a year, but means a day.
Racked high up against the walls
diamond patterned cardigans,
golf motif pullovers, sky-dark trousers,
football shirts with embroidered logos,
all hang like triple XL moults
waiting to squeeze onto new life,
while underneath log dug-out shoes
curl into shadow along the carpet's edge.
"He can't hear you," boss brother shouts,
"his ears are just solar panels for his lips."
I smile at this pellet from the cross-fire
of incessant call and response,
but just a stifled crack of the face,
nothing like the jaw-loose, addicted gape
they all manage hundreds of times
in each of their thousands and thousands
of chalked out, end-on blokey days.

I see them all with a laugh on sometimes
heading towards the car park at six,
the quick jerk of their unified gait
strobing the headlights of passing cars,
on their way home to wives and mothers
or whoever else it is who maintains
such new men for that inherited world.
As I edge my way out of the shop
I'm snared near denim by an almost-wink,
can feel the gravity of coming spiel.
"The original indigo Wrangler shirt, sir,"
the retro-Sixties one in his twenties says,
"pearl stud fasteners, peaked yokes,
a rodeo style worth thinking about."
His large blue eyes pull away slowly
with that confidential, sidelong look
that can seed a paranoia, and then I'm free,
stepping across their ages-worn rubber mat,
its huge indented twin footprints,
as if a Sasquatch had passed that way,
or something else much larger than life.

Nobody Dies

I come across you for the first time
smiling and holding Chinese hands
on page 39 of a Saturday Guardian.
It is the obituary page and you fill it, almost
with a life so wide and long and deep
that it has lost the truth of its own age.

You were 80 or thereabouts, Ta Mok,
born into Buddhism and well-off peasantry,
your real name still a subject for debate.
Of these things only you knew the truth,
small clarities you denied a patient world
from which once you pulled so many.

Hot tempered, cocksure and arrogant
you never let them see your Napoleon,
cultivating the power of parochialism,
sowing in the strength of true family.
You got lucky by being number 3,
big enough to kill, small enough to live.

Your need to sack and burn and kill
was just the resistance warrior's way,
and you commanded the way so well.
When one time your leg took a bullet
the limb was hacked off and you fought on:
they don't come much harder than that.

Later, after the evacuation of Phnom Penh,
the fields, the skulls counted from 0,
you purged the armies on Pol's paranoia.
3 decades forward, before your final coma,
a lawyer instructs the world to know
you only planted rice, built bridges, dams.

In the paper's photograph from 1975
you sport the idiot cap of the proletarian,
wallow amidst comrades' peasant uniformity,
are ecstatic in the grasp of your puppeteers.
Mass murderer is your final epithet:
this is an educated age, you out of time.

Shallow Grave

I won't give you a new home
and a trigger-happy retirement.

No, when I don't want you anymore,
when you freeze once too often
or leave me hanging just a little too long,
I'll take you into the garage,
hack you up with a shovel
(Spear and Jackson, toughened steel)
and let your hard drive really know
who wears the words in my house.

I'll put your bits into carrier bags,
mix them with ordinary household waste,
deposit half at the local tip
and half in some randomly selected skip
in Macclesfield or Stoke.

Then I'll go out and buy myself another.

Babbage Hardcore

'*In 1814 Georgiana Wolryche-Whitmore of Dudmaston married a young mathematician named Charles Babbage*' – Shropshire Tourism

There's this girl I see who likes sweeping,
who pushes her broom and pan-on-a-stick
all around the floor of a coffee shop,
her head down, her hair falling, her vision

mapping and netting a terrain of crumbs
with the fail-safe instinct of satellite eyes.
I imagine her on these grey scullery steps,
a cold stone leading from the maids' entrance,

the great house dividing above her into halls.
Babbage is still about his plumbing scheme,
kicking up dust as he hardwires a heart
of warmth to vent through every living space.

Later that morning Lady WW will apologise
to the housekeeper for his eccentricities,
confide his intolerance of drunkenness,
the perpetual occurrence of broken panes,

a hurdy-gurdy racket common to the street.
She will ask about the demure weepiness
of the help she passes sometimes at work,
her connection to a local farrier brute.

This girl I see likes to sweep and cash up,
presses close to the till at a shift's end
nodding the purr of paper rolling through,
its number friction kindling at her belly.

Outside the coffee shop hip hop hammers air
each time her boyfriend pulls up on the dot,
fellow staff waving, then slagging him off
as Tupac beats and tattoos steal her away.

Who Do You Think You Are?

I google your name and of course you appear,
pages and pages of people you could never be.

I do this now and again throughout the year
when empty, wandering moments at my PC
cause me to check the web's ever widening
for some stub of your life on this planet.
Two decades on loss is a wholesome thing,
not some wrapped wail or numb sentiment.

The river still floods to your old work place,
and the children you never came to know
spent teen lives in that nearby drinking hole.
My son has your hypochondria and impatience,
my two daughters your tick and knitted brow;
and none are subtle when drunk, or on a roll.

A Father's Trousers

The holiday was difficult, you coming back
into family after the abyss of an affair,
dutifully sacking her off for a final crack
at married life with kids who didn't care
a toss how it went. In a Paris pension
for a week we all shared that rotten
breath of a room's basin and the tension
of those casual slacks in checked cotton.

Outmoded but durable you'd packed them
for a renaissance only to find legs shorter
than anticipated the first morning, their hem
riding your socks through the Latin Quarter.
Every fifty yards you'd turn to us and ask
for reassurance, then stride on at half mast.

Driving Back Home I Remember Wicklow

September is a difficult month, bipolar
in its shutting down, its storing up,
how it stacks the fields
with memorable, un-recallable light.
For you the early Seventies
may have been like this,
beginning again by going back.

A bum-fluff gooseberry
for a fortnight
in your shot at a new life
I liked her on our holiday,
the smell she left in rooms,
how she felt the fool in me.
I indulged the literary tours, too
in the spirit of the father:
Joyce's Martello Tower,
Yeats' Thoor Ballylee,
Synge's *Playboy* at the Abbey.

Our cottage was green wood,
full of early light,
and mealtimes facing mountain
were always a time
for thoughts to loosen.
I remember her Irish Stew,
talked up by you for days,
its butter beans
and bones of greasy lamb
puddled, uneatable, on my plate.

Dirty Car

I never clean my car: weeks, months, years
of nose to tail road spume
have made it the trusty, caked tonsil
I have come to know and love.

One summer an egg fell from a tree
and fried on the bonnet for a fortnight.
Its amoebic shadow is a distinguishing mark.

Sometimes the woman next door
offers me her power hose,
says it can scour slabs,
is fierce enough to bring a fence down.

She comes out in trackies most Sundays
to Dyson her Megane's upholstery
while impressing a music taste on the street.

When I say no to the hose
she offers me wax, or a bucket of suds.

Distance Learning

He knows about his kids in unusual ways.

Once they wrote to him in school reports,
addressed envelopes in class,
sent them with a pocket money stamp.
Their paragraphs told of influential things,
appetites that hungered,
fads that flared, then faded.

He is a Bank Holiday palm reader,
some hippy seer on the margins
gleaning personality from moon and stars,
the swirls and slant of written words.

Blessed

Perhaps not achieving is a skill, a gift.

He sometimes felt he had achieved nothing
in a quiet, bad tempered way,
had stood each year in late October sun
basking in nothingness

nothingness born of recollections
of the last basking,
the longer end-day shadows
filling up a lawn again uncut for winter.

Before & After

Before the age of 40
- open brackets,
fortyinletters,
close brackets -
he thought constantly
about sex
and ways to be clever.

After the age of 40
(forty)
he thinks constantly
about death
and ways he's been stupid.

Somewhere South

This town was an overcast bush
for three work-away days in April.
Now, after bullet rain, there is some sky.

The trains drop orderly into their silos here,
they approach the grid of departure platforms
after reasonable delays and leave with alibis
towards a curve of steel-braced scrub.

Well heeled schoolgirls engross on benches,
guards with leather bags and red peaked hats
prepare towards unfinished work tasks.
The cappuccino bar advertises apple pastries,
lists its bargain buys on a little blackboard.

Beyond the passenger assistance room
grassed-in tracks serve nowhere.
Over a wire fence the *Bamboo Garden*
waits to do take-aways on a soft street,
a tree like ornamental twigs in a floor vase
has found the climate, is coming into green.

Entitlement

Everyone needs a scam, a hustle,
some slack at the work margins
where they can get a little peace.

Not being a smoker
I righteously crave to stand
at the building's dullest doorway,
ignoring everyone and everything
save the distant sucked shingle
of traffic's ebb and flow,
to feel the day's exterior,
its ozone-bitten, bare sensibility.

Sometimes there is sun
on wheelie bin plastic,
a bright dandelion in tarmac's dirt.

No one else comes. It is my door.

Escalator

Once I feared your polished, even teeth,
thought they'd love a bite of *Startrite* soles.

Now on grey, wrung-out days
you lift me beyond perfumed lab coats,
up through menswear's indifferent rim
to a sky-lit decorum of table service,
hot tea and fresh milk in a jug.

You unmake hallways, landings, stairwells,
those nothing spaces of our lives
fit only for scuttling and fretting in.

And on the way back down
I bull my brogues with your brushes.

Gap

After rumours about a planning scam
for a fancy piazza by the market
the official word was concrete cancer.
Hired hydraulics pecked its sinewed blocks
to a corner of hose dampened dust,
all six storeys of the brute gone in weeks,
the unthinkable slaughter of a work-life routine.

Municipal monolith damming the west of the city,
it knew me intimately, took my car daily:
knackered lift, stairwell of piss,
landings you couldn't swing a Kwik Save carrier in,
puddled levels with no reg above a K,
warnings of the week felt-tipped
onto cardboard pieces left to litter the barriers.

A fag fumed plastic hut clocked the years,
reached into my world with tattooed arm
or bar brawl glance
for dirt-grained, recycled tickets
thumped from a cut-price council system;
sometimes, by arrangement, let me stay late
parked close to paint and rubber streaked bollards.

On Harrison & Dearborn

I was on the corner of Harrison and Dearborn
when I heard the news. Starbucks, about four-thirty.
The young server detected my accent,
said "I'm really sorry what happened to you guys,"
and I must have looked dumbfounded or pale
because after he'd told me about London
he quickly apologised for spoiling my day.
I parted the staring queue behind me
and drank my iced latte at a window counter.
Outside an Asian teenager in a tight T shirt
paced up and down in the warm lake wind
smoking and talking on his mobile phone;
a green US Mail relay box stood fixed in shadow.
Inside, jazz circulated along the air conditioning.

Change

The train noses up a curve of rail,
packs itself into the station.
I don't recognise you at first -
shorter hair, new colour, nose stud -
but when I do you are a balsa person
moving towards me in a crowd of iron.

It has been six days since we talked
and it will only be the same again.
I give you the bag with all the things
you asked me to bring -
photographs, earrings, underwear -
and as we wait the eleven minutes
for your connection in the wet sun
it is as if we are looking at each other
in a fairground hall of mirrors.

Then you take your thinness onto the train
and its longness takes you away.

Young Girl Alone

I realise later I could have gone inside
with the book-huggers
sipping through their froth
in the warm
and that she, too, could have done the same.
Instead she sat at a round metal table
by the entrance
passed by everyone at least twice
like the stone lion and its *welcome* necklace
of poker-worked wood.
With feathered, end-coloured hair
and in rib-hugging top and jeans
she leaned cross legged over her tea
nursing a loneliness of style.

When the chill of spring afternoon shadow
forced me to scrape my chair
against grey flagstones and leave
she remained sitting,
flicking and relighting her roll-up.
Twenty minutes later
when I passed again the alley
that leads to the café from the street
she was still there,
as if at the end of a telescope,
and as I crossed the light she looked up,
as you might have done.

Tell It How It Is

He's been cheated, short changed
in his portfolio of life events.

He thinks it would be nice sometimes
to tell of a breakdown,
a fortuitously foiled suicide attempt,
the bright, near-death tunnel of light
that jerked him bolt upright one day
against a thousand quid a week habit;
but this has passed him by,
like the identity crisis,
the drink problem,
the meat-money-gone-to-horses shame
that didn't happen and can't be told.

Nobody has ever talked him down
from an overwhelming desire to quit,
reasoned from his resolute hand
the fervent match of devastation.
True, he can manage the odd spiel
about the Child Support Agency,
a tale or two about estate agents,
but how does he live without epiphany?

He feels a fraud if he just says
that each day's bric-a-brac
of movement, light and noise
is the moment's pain-free gift;
but he says it like that anyway
and trusts in time some doctor,
that revered judge of mortal passage,
will visit his bed-ridden, limp body
and tell him straight to his face
what he thinks he already knows:

it hasn't been easy living his life.

Six Notes

Moving wax-like
into safe vessels
we become our parents

Flats rising
from across a hidden park -
white electrical goods

Blown scalped palm
fixed scrawny succulent -
holiday pool views

Truths untightened
flying upwards out of reach -
ripcord scenario

Theme bar at forty–
afternoon light doubly fades
through tinted glass

Late October sun –
gentleness on the face
water in the eyes

Dwellings

Sixty seven was the year of setting free,
final eviction from a sideshow family life
serving teas from a kitchen in a cave.
After that day trippers out walking the Edge
could no longer stop to meet the Flintstones,
ponder a world deep beyond their window.

No more generations rocking in the hole,
winding the deep well in apron or smock.
No more tinted memories in black and white
of smoky winter warmth and airy summer cool.
No sail-flap of laundry on the roof terrace,
no place for scythe or besom against a wall.

The Seventies ruined Holy Austin for real.
Without guardians she regressed, lost her grip,
let vandals in to ruminate and urinate,
to smoke out and litter out her lonely rooms.
They only made the most of what they found:
house to cave, rock to wreck, dust again to dust.

Lucretia, Benjamin, Thomas, Sarah, John,
all of the names and their earth-honest trades
have gone forever, won't live there anymore.
But postcard perfect rehab still leaves room
for history's penknife on red-stone walls:
ban the bomb, a heart; Kenny, Sandra, England.

Outings

I

We spend
our first

day away
wringing

out and
wrestling

down the
iniquity

of words
spoken

and thoughts
unsaid.

We agree
the next

trip be
silence.

II

From silences
we construct

edifices
of words

that burst
the skin

of sentence
and rise

away from
reason.

These pyramids
were once

phonecalls,
this sphinx

a remark's
stare.

Personal Stuff

There is a place where your loves meet,
where all of them rub each other up
in dark, quiet stillness.

Under its single spring-loaded clip
art house cards forgive the cuteness
of Muppet and mutant mouse
shaping those tranquil after-thoughts.
As if in a warm after dinner kiss
the taste of their words mingle.

That is where the years are reckoned,
lives and places and circumstance
plundered for fidelity that is yours alone.

A heaven may be like that box file,
collecting close near-forgotten parts
that once claimed the same name.

Day Trip

I walk the pier's planks
over green sea,
stand rodless
where others come to fish.
In the near haze
wind turbines go about
their slow, tactless pilates
while back along the beach
I can still see the child
who was digging holes,
who stood squealing
at a rim of kelp-tea froth.

Later I walk up a track
to the camera obscura,
find it closed, shuttered up,
the wide bay of its view
out of season
stretched out below.

What is this dumb surprise,
the un-remembering
in a town less open?
The gulls sling their bellies low
from guest house gutters,
bully the air
with something maudlin,
something far too loud.

Audit Team

He trawls spreadsheets for days,
his jacket on the back
of someone's orthopaedic chair,
by mid morning a white shirt
pulled open at the neck.
Fingers poke the keyboard,
ribbons of evidence
track his watering eyes.
He gropes for the guest mug
we fill four times a day
with an own brand instant.

She is next door. Her laugh
is like one you might hear
through a hotel room wall at night,
girlie, a little beyond control,
one that could be hopelessness,
or love.

Final Frame

When I see this guy outside the Odeon
smoking an urgent cigarette
I think of how I'd take up the habit again
if the Earth was doomed,
in the path of a fireball say,
and how there'd be nothing hurried
about my last smoke,
no frantic, hollow cheeked pulling
or quick-fire suck and blow
into the damp night,
the hastened tip elongated
to a glowing hornet's body,
the white shaft egged on to brown
by thumb flicks and stares.
No, I'd retrieve a packet mid-sentence
from a deep trouser pocket,
take a foil-fresh, tight tobacco stick
straight to the lips
and sizzle its end to life
with the snap of a gold Zippo.
Because great minds think alike
my friend would be ahead of me,
a deep gasp already streaming nostrils,
chopping from his mouth
with each burst of a short little laugh.
It would be the end of the world, you see,
and we would see the humour in it all,
an irony only the comfort of nicotine
and occupied fingers allows.
We'd chat and exchange glances,
our words unimportant
compared to the length of ash between puffs,
the real and only point of everything.

I'd be just where it starts to get tar-hot
when the fireball incinerated Earth,
and my friend may either have tossed his
or be holding its butt between teeth
as he steadied the scene
with both hands
in the frame of our disposable camera.

Notes

Lapworth Museum is in the grounds of Birmingham University and contains a unique collection of rocks and fossils.

Brindley Place is in Birmingham, just off Broad Street.

Ta Mok, referred to in 'Nobody Dies', was a Khymer Rouge leader nicknamed 'The Butcher', who died in 2006 in Cambodia.

Dudmaston House, referred to in 'Babbage Hardcore', is a country estate in Quatt, Shropshire.

Harrison and Dearborn are streets in Chicago, USA.

The Holy Austin Rock Houses referred to in 'Dwellings' are in Kinver, South Staffordshire and in the trust of English Heritage.